Managing Editor
Karen Goldfluss, M.S. Ed.

Editor-in-Chief
Sharon Coan, M.S. Ed.

Illustrator
Renée Christine Yates

Cover Artist
Barb Lorseyedi

Art Manager
Kevin Barnes

Art Director
CJae Froshay

Imaging
Rosa C. See

Product Manager
Phil Garcia

Publisher
Mary D. Smith, M.S. Ed.

Full Color **Grades 1-2**

Literacy Activities

Science

Teacher Created Resources

Author

Lorin Klistoff, M.A.

Teacher Created Resources

Teacher Created Resources, Inc.
6421 Industry Way
Westminster, CA 92683
www.teachercreated.com

ISBN-0-7439-3171-8

©2004 Teacher Created Resources, Inc.
Reprinted, 2005
Made in U.S.A.

Table of Contents

Introduction

Literacy Activities: Science is a wonderful addition to any first or second grade science curriculum. This book was created especially for the busy teachers of young students. The hands-on, developmentally appropriate activities are sure to provide your students with fun-filled learning experiences. The activities are full-color and will add some spice to the regular classroom material. The contents in the book provide a variety of ways to reinforce science concepts and skills while maintaining student interest. The activities are easy to implement with little or no preparation at all. The activities are meant to support and be a resource for teachers as they teach these content skills. The activities provide review and practice in the following areas of science:

- five senses and how they help us learn
- living and nonliving things
- plant parts and their functions
- different environments or habitats of plants and animals
- different characteristics of animals
- life cycle of a plant, frog, or butterfly
- basic functions of the different parts of the human body
- water cycle
- the sequence of seasons and what activities happen in each season
- how fossils are made and how scientists collect fossils
- different kinds of dinosaurs and what facts scientists have learned about them
- natural resources that are used by people
- solids, liquids, and gases
- magnets
- sink and float

Each activity is set up with an easy-to-follow lesson. First, each lesson states the objective or learning skill and the materials needed. Most of the materials are provided inside this book. Next, the lesson outlines in what kinds of groupings the activity can be implemented. Most of the activities can be adapted in multiple ways and can be "custom tailored." They can be implemented as a whole-class lesson, small group, partners, independently, or in a science center. The activities can also be adapted for a variety of student levels. Suggestions are listed in the actual directions of the activity or they are suggested in the "Ideas" section. The "Ideas" section contains many helpful hints on such things as storage of materials or ideas to either enhance or extend the activity. Overall, the book is an asset to any first or second grade teacher.

Making Sense of It All

 Skill

- Identify the five senses and how they help us learn

 Student Grouping

- partners
- small group
- whole group
- center

 Materials

- chalkboard or whiteboard
- chalk or whiteboard markers
- Five Senses Cards (pages 11, 13, and 15)
- Five Senses Gameboard (pages 8 and 9) if playing option *b* (See below in Directions #5.)
- a playing marker for each student if playing option *b* (See below in Directions #5.)
- Answer Key (page 5)

 Directions

1. Explain to students that there are five senses that help us learn about things: sight, smell, touch, hearing, and taste. Draw a picture on the board for each sense as you are naming them (sight–eyes, smell–nose, touch–hand, hearing–ear, taste–tongue).

2. Brainstorm with students examples of each sense.

3. Tell them that they will be playing a Five Senses game.

4. Mix up the Five Senses Cards and place them in a pile facedown.

5. You have two options of playing this game: (a) As a whole group, you or a student may pick a card and read it to the whole class. The students have to guess what sense it is. (b) In a center, partners, or small group, place markers for each player on the Five Senses Gameboard on the area where it says, "START." Have each player pick a card and guess which of the five senses the card is illustrating. If his or her guess is correct, he or she may move the marker down the path to the sense on the board that is illustrated on the card. Tell him or her to follow the path to "FINISH." If the pile of cards is finished, remix them and place the pile facedown and use them again.

6. Check answers with the Answer Key.

 Ideas

- Laminate gameboard and cards, especially when using in a center.
- Have a variety of objects with which students can explore using their five senses.

Answer Key

Seeing

 What a beautiful rainbow!

 The painting is so pretty.

 The flowers are red and yellow.

 There is a picture of Mom.

 The poster has a monster on it.

 The ocean looks so beautiful.

 The clouds are white.

 Look at the bird in the tree.

Hearing

 The telephone is ringing.

 I like this song on the radio.

 That drum is too loud!

 The car engine is noisy.

 Somebody is banging the pots.

 The car's horn is beeping.

 The dog is barking.

 Someone is knocking on the door.

Feeling

 The tub of water is too cold.

 The cat's fur feels so soft.

 That rock is smooth.

 The floor is slippery.

 The sand is hot!

 The ride was bumpy.

 The chair is hard.

 The bed is nice to sleep in.

Tasting

 This ice cream tastes great!

 The candy is too sweet.

 This pickle is too sour!

 The pretzel is salty.

 The lollipop is good.

 The hamburger is tasty.

 The orange is juicy.

 The lemon is sour.

Smelling

 The soup smells so good!

 The trash stinks!

 The perfume is nice.

 Something smells like smoke.

 I smell a skunk.

 It smells like a rose.

 My dog smells bad.

 The coffee smells good.

#3171 Science Literacy Activities

#3171 Science Literacy Activities

Five

START

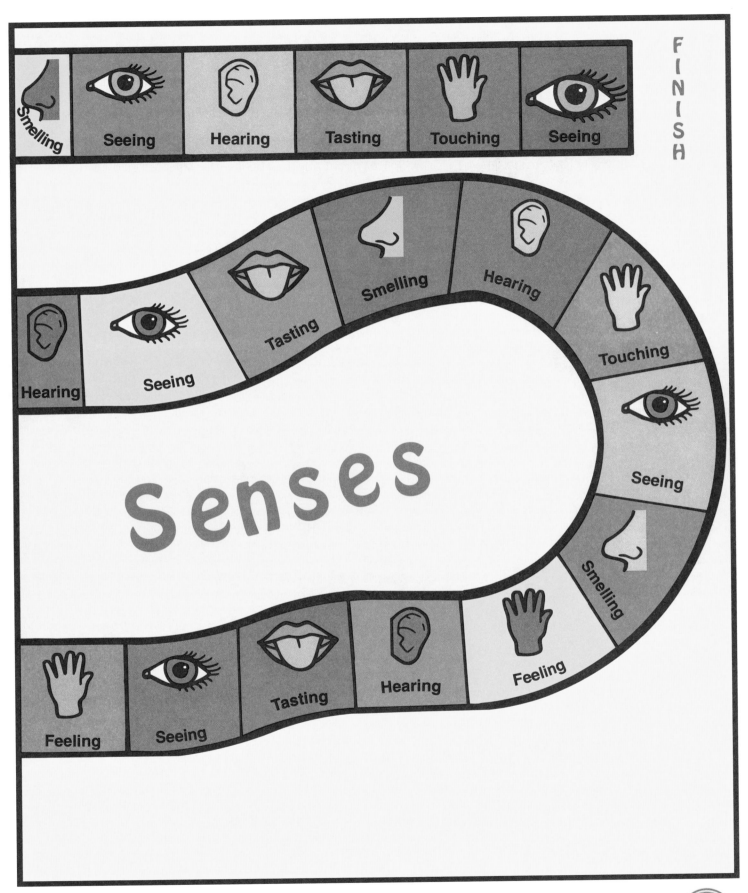

#3171 Science Literacy Activities   *©Teacher Created Resources, Inc.*

Five Senses Cards

What a beautiful rainbow!

The telephone is ringing.

The painting is so pretty.

I like this song on the radio.

The flowers are red and yellow.

That drum is too loud!

There is a picture of Mom.

The car engine is noisy.

The poster has a monster on it.

Somebody is banging the pots.

The ocean looks so beautiful.

The car's horn is beeping.

The clouds are white.

The dog is barking.

Look at the bird in the tree.

#3171 Science Literacy Activities

Five Senses Cards

Someone is knocking
on the door.

The tub of water is too cold.

This ice cream tastes great!

The cat's fur feels so soft.

The candy is too sweet.

That rock is smooth.

This pickle is too sour!

The floor is slippery.

The pretzel is salty.

The sand is hot!

The lollipop is good.

The ride was bumpy.

The hamburger is tasty.

The chair is hard.

The orange is juicy.

13

Five Senses Cards

The bed is nice to sleep in.

The lemon is sour.

The soup smells so good!

The trash stinks!

The perfume is nice.

Something smells like smoke.

I smell a skunk.

It smells like a rose.

My dog smells bad.

The coffee smells good.

Schoolyard Sort

Skill

- Differentiate between living and nonliving things

Student Grouping
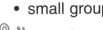

- whole group
- small group
- partners
- center
- independent

Materials

- chalkboard or whiteboard
- chalk or whiteboard markers
- sorting mats (pages 20 and 21)
- Living and Nonliving Cards (pages 23 and 25)
- Answer Key (page 18)
- tape

Directions

1. Write the words *Living* and *Nonliving* on the board.
2. Point to the word *Living*. Tell students that living things need food, water, and air. Tell them that living things grow.
3. Then point to the word *Nonliving*. Tell students that nonliving things do not need food, water, and air.
4. Ask students to brainstorm some living and nonliving things and discuss which category each would fall under.
5. Write each idea under the appropriate title.
6. Mix up the Living and Nonliving Cards. Have students sort the cards. You may choose to sort in the following ways: (a) Tape the sorting mats on the board. As a whole class, tape each living or nonliving card under the appropriate category. Copy a Living and Nonliving sorting mat for each student. Have them write each word under the appropriate category as you are taping the card on the board. For instance, if you are taping a boat under Nonliving, have students write the word *boat* on their papers titled *Nonliving*. You may wish to have them draw pictures by the words. (b) Make copies of the sorting mats and cards for each student and have them sort independently. (c) Place mats and cards in a center for students to sort. (*Note:* Make a copy of the Answer Key on page 18 for students to check their answers.)

Ideas

- Laminate sorting mats and cards for durability, especially if using in a center.
- Have students make additional cards for the sorting mats.
- Make a book cover titled, *Living Things*, and another book cover titled, *Nonliving Things*. Have students create pages for each book. For example, one student could draw a picture of a caterpillar. He or she could label it *caterpillar* and write some describing words on the page. Then add it to the book, titled *Living Things*. When all student pages are finished, bind the book together and add it to the class library.
- Have students cut pictures out of magazines and make a collage of living and nonliving things.

Answer Key

Living Things

 tree

 butterfly

 girl

 ant

 ladybug

 worm

 bird

 flower

 teacher

 grass

 squirrel

 cat

Nonliving Things

 rock

 jump rope

 lunchbox

 trash can

 table

 bell

 swing

 water

 paper

 ball

 whistle

 penny

#3171 Science Literacy Activities

Living Things

Nonliving Things

Living Things (Cards)

tree

ant

bird

grass

butterfly

ladybug

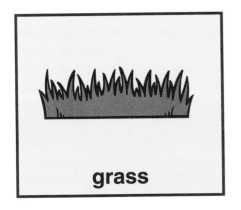

flower

squirrel

girl

worm

teacher

cat

#3171 Science Literacy Activities

Nonliving Things (Cards)

rock

trash can

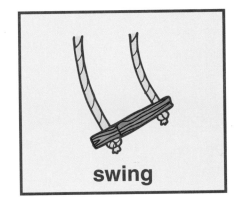

swing

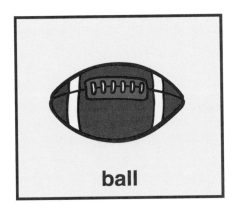

ball

jump rope

table

water

whistle

lunchbox

bell

paper

penny

#3171 Science Literacy Activities

Plant Puzzler

 Skill

- Identify the parts of a plant and their functions

 Student Grouping

- independently
- small group

- large group
- center

 Materials

- Parts of a Plant diagram (pages 30 and 31)
- Plant Puzzler Cards (page 33)

- Answer Key (page 28)

 Directions

1. Remind students of the things that plants need to grow: light, air, and water.
2. Post the plant diagram where all students can view it.
3. Tell students that plants have different parts that have special jobs.
4. Read the words together on the diagram.
5. Tell students that they will be listening to riddles about the different parts of the plant. They will have to guess what part of the plant answers the riddle. Tell them to raise their hands if they think they know the answer. (*Option:* You may want to break students into teams. Or, if students are doing this independently at a center, have them copy the number of the puzzler, the question, and their answers on a piece of paper. Have them use the answer key to correct their papers.)
6. Read Plant Puzzler 1.
7. Have students guess until the correct answer is given. Give encouraging comments to incorrect answers, such as "That's a good try." (*Note:* If playing in teams, encourage students to have a discussion and come to a conclusion together. If one team arrives at the incorrect answer, the question is then given to the other team. You may want to keep a tally of points, one point for every correct answer.)
8. Continue until all riddles are solved. (*Note:* Check answers with Answer Key.)

 Ideas

- Laminate the diagram of the plant and the cards for durability, especially if using in a center.
- Read some plant books or grow a plant prior to starting the activity.
- Bring a variety of plants and seeds. Have students compare the similarities and differences between the plants, such as the shapes of the leaves or shapes of their seeds.
- Have students bring in various vegetables that they eat. Identify the parts of vegetable. Then have a discussion about what part of the plant they eat. (Example: carrot = root)
- As a challenge, add more vocabulary to the diagram, such as *stamen*, *stigma*, or *style*. Add more riddle cards to match the diagram.

Answer Key

Plant Puzzler 1: root

Plant Puzzler 2: root

Plant Puzzler 3: leaf

Plant Puzzler 4: stem

Plant Puzzler 5: stem

Plant Puzzler 6: flower

Plant Puzzler 7: seed coat

Plant Puzzler 8: seedling

Plant Puzzler 9: seedling or seed

Plant Puzzler 10: petal

Plant Puzzler 11: bud

Plant Puzzler 12: sepal

#3171 Science Literacy Activities

Parts of a Plant

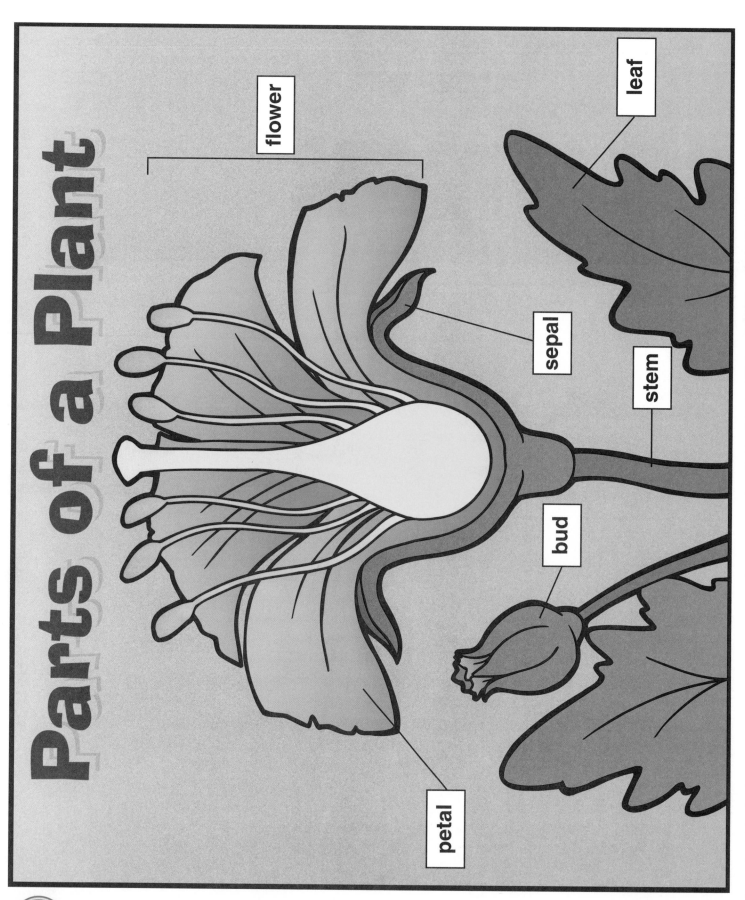

leaf

flower

sepal

stem

bud

petal

#3171 Science Literacy Activities

©Teacher Created Resources, Inc.

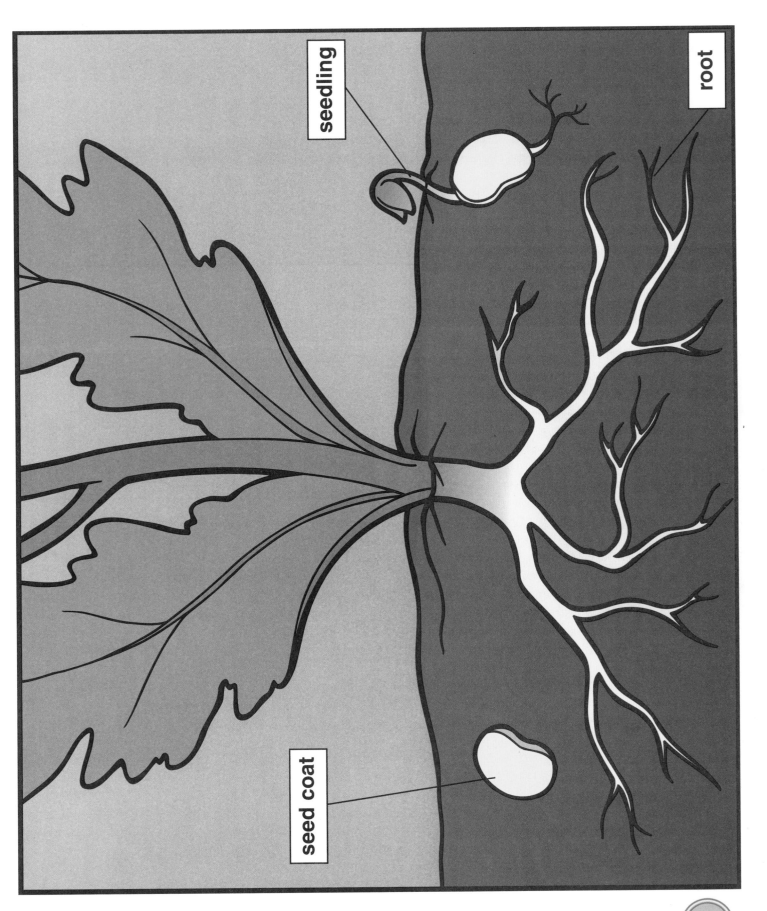

#3171 Science Literacy Activities

©*Teacher Created Resources, Inc.*

Plant Puzzler Cards

Plant Puzzler 1
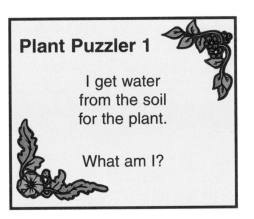

I get water
from the soil
for the plant.

What am I?

Plant Puzzler 2

I help hold
the plant
in the soil.

What am I?

Plant Puzzler 3
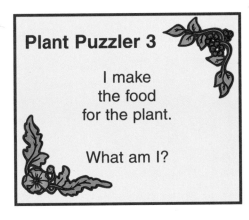

I make
the food
for the plant.

What am I?

Plant Puzzler 4

I hold up the
plant's leaves
and flower.

What am I?

Plant Puzzler 5

I carry water
and nutrients
to the leaves.

What am I?

Plant Puzzler 6
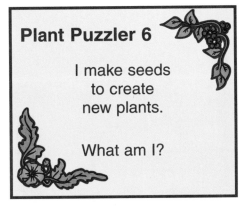

I make seeds
to create
new plants.

What am I?

Plant Puzzler 7

I am a covering
that protects
the seed.

What am I?

Plant Puzzler 8
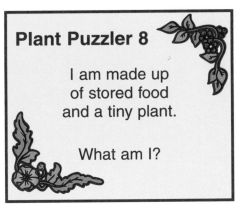

I am made up
of stored food
and a tiny plant.

What am I?

Plant Puzzler 9

A new, tiny plant
grows out
of me.

What am I?

Plant Puzzler 10
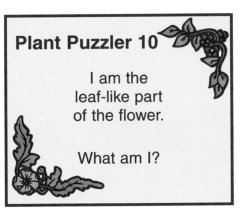

I am the
leaf-like part
of the flower.

What am I?

Plant Puzzler 11
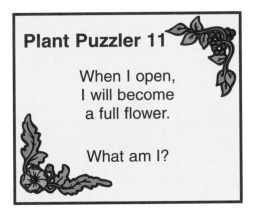

When I open,
I will become
a full flower.

What am I?

Plant Puzzler 12
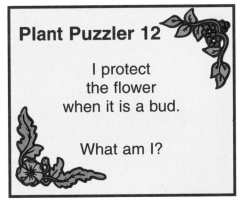

I protect
the flower
when it is a bud.

What am I?

#3171 Science Literacy Activities

Where's My Home?

 Skill

- Classify plants and animals in different environments or habitats

 Student Grouping

- whole group
- small group
- center
- partners
- independent

 Materials

- chalkboard or whiteboard
- chalk or whiteboard markers
- Connect the pages of the scenes of each environment. (ocean on pages 40 and 41, desert on pages 44 and 45, forest on pages 48 and 49, and rain forest on pages 52 and 53)
- Animal and Plant Cards from each environment (ocean on page 55, desert on page 57, forest on page 59, and rain forest on page 61)
- Answer Key (page 37)

 Directions

1. Write the words *ocean*, *desert*, *forest*, and *rain forest* on the board.
2. Explain each of the environments: ocean (a large body of salt water), desert (a dry place with lots of sunlight and very little rain), forest (a place where many trees grow) and rain forest (a place that is wet all year and has many trees).
3. Ask students to brainstorm any plants or animals they know that live in each environment.
4. Lay each habitat scene on the floor or post on a wall.
5. Mix up the animal and plant cards from the different habitats.
6. Tell students that today they will sort plants and animals into their correct habitats. Read the animal or plant name and the card fact, and then ask students to find the appropriate habitat. For example, "Jellyfish—I have an umbrella-shaped body and a stinger that can hurt humans. Where do you think the jellyfish lives? Ocean? Desert? Forest? Or a rain forest?" Place or post the jellyfish card on the ocean scene.
7. Give students the animal and plant cards to sort independently, with partners, as a small group, or sort as a whole class.
8. Check the Answer Key for answers.

Ideas

- Laminate the boards and cards for durability.
- Have students develop more cards of animals and plants that inhabit the same environment.
- Have students choose two animals or two plants from different environments and make comparisons. (Example: the fennec fox from the desert and the red fox from the forest)
- Make books for each environment. Have students create a page for each book that includes an animal or plant from that environment.
- Have students go through magazines and make collages for each habitat.
- Use the cards and scenes to develop decorative bulletin boards.

Answer Key

Ocean Animals and Plants

 starfish
 jellyfish

 bottlenose dolphin
 octopus

 sea turtle
 kelp

 squid
 coral

 great white shark
 algae

 lobster
 red anemone

Desert Animals and Plants

 sidewinder
 roadrunner

 camel
 desert tortoise

 black-tailed jack rabbit
 thorny devil lizard

 kangaroo rat
 Joshua tree

 fennec fox
 beavertail cactus

 cactus wren
 yucca

Forest Animals and Plants

 elk
 tawny owl

 moose
 woodpecker

 skunk
 red fox

 eastern chipmunk
 mountain laurel

 black bear
 mountain berry bush

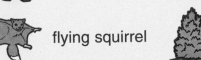 flying squirrel
Scotch pine

Rain Forest Animals and Plants

 mandrill
 toucan

 Eclectus parrot
 cacao tree

 jaguar
 rubber plant

 macaw
 orchid

 red-eyed tree frog
 kapok tree

 orangutan
 bamboo

#3171 Science Literacy Activities

#3171 Science Literacy Activities

©Teacher Created Resources, Inc.

#3171 Science Literacy Activities

Ocean

Desert

#3171 Science Literacy Activities

#3171 Science Literacy Activities

©*Teacher Created Resources, Inc.*

47

Forest

#3171 Science Literacy Activities

#3171 Science Literacy Activities

©*Teacher Created Resources, Inc.*

Rain Forest

starfish

My shape helps me wrap myself around food.

bottlenose dolphin

My fins and tail help me swim fast to catch food.

sea turtle

I have flippers that help me steer.

squid

I squirt "ink" so I can get away from my enemy.

great white shark

I am the largest fish that hunts.

lobster

I have a hard shell and have eight walking legs.

jellyfish

I have an umbrella-shaped body and stingers that can hurt humans.

octopus

I have eight arms covered with suckers, and I eat shellfish.

kelp

I am a giant seaweed that grows in the cool waters.

coral

I am an animal that lives in big groups in a coral reef.

algae

We are small plants that live in water.

red anemone

My tentacles have stinging cells to help me catch food.

Desert Animals and Plants

sidewinder

I move my body sideways in the hot sand.

camel

I can go a long time without water.

black-tailed jack rabbit

I have powerful back legs to help me jump away from enemies.

kangaroo rat

I store plant seeds deep in my burrow.

fennec fox

I have big ears to keep me cool.

cactus wren

I make my nest on the cactus plant.

roadrunner

I run very fast to catch snakes and lizards.

desert tortoise

I live on land and have a domed shell.

thorny devil lizard

I can change colors so it is easier for me to hide.

Joshua tree

I have spiky leaves and have a fruit which is food for desert animals.

beavertail cactus

I have thorns to keep animals from eating me.

yucca

I have thick leaves to hold water.

#3171 Science Literacy Activities

Forest Animals and Plants

elk

I eat grass by using my sharp teeth.

moose

I am the largest of all living deer.

skunk

My terrible smell helps keep away intruders.

eastern chipmunk

I carry nuts in my mouth to store in my burrow for the winter.

black bear

I sleep through the winter and wake up in the spring to eat.

flying squirrel

I can glide in the air from tree to tree.

tawny owl

I hunt at night and make hooting sounds.

woodpecker

I have a strong beak for making holes in tree trunks for nests.

red fox

During the night I hunt for food, and I live in burrows.

mountain laurel

I am a small tree with white and purple flowers.

mountain berry bush

I need less sunlight than trees.

Scotch pine

My leaves are needles, and my bark is thick at my trunk.

#3171 Science Literacy Activities

Rain Forest Animals and Plants

mandrill

I am one of the largest of all monkeys.

Eclectus parrot

My colors help me hide from my enemy.

jaguar
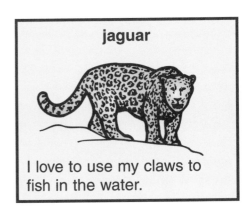
I love to use my claws to fish in the water.

macaw

I live near the treetops, and my beak can open the hardest of fruits.

red-eyed tree frog

I am a frog with bright, red eyes.

orangutan

I live most of my life in the tops of trees.

toucan

I have a huge, colorful beak.

cacao tree

I grow beans used to make chocolate.

rubber plant

I am used to make things like rubber bands.

orchid
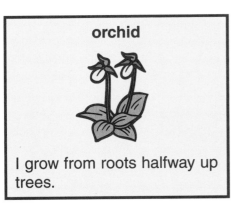
I grow from roots halfway up trees.

kapok tree

I am a very large tree and home for many animals.

bamboo

I am from the grass family and used to build many things.

Characteristic Classification

 Skill

- Classify animals according to characteristics

 Student Grouping

- whole group
- small group
- partners
- independent
- center

 Materials

- chalkboard or whiteboard
- chalk or whiteboard markers
- chart and matching cards (pages 65–69 or pages 71–73)
- Answer Key (page 64)

 Directions

1. Tell students that all animals are alike in that they all need food, water, air, and a place to live.

2. Explain to students that animals can also be put into different groups.

3. Write the following vocabulary on the board, depending on what chart you want to use. (For page 65, write the words *mammal*, *reptile*, *amphibian*, *insect*, *bird*, and *fish*. If using the chart on page 71, then write the words *vertebrates* and *invertebrates*.)

4. Explain each of the vocabulary words.

5. Ask students to brainstorm some animals that might fit in each category.

6. Mix up the cards.

7. Have students sort the cards under the appropriate headings. (*Note:* Check answers with Answer Key.)

Ideas

- Laminate cards and charts, especially if using in a center.
- Have students make their own charts and list other animals that were not included in the card set.
- Have students create a science dictionary and add words such as *amphibian*, *invertebrate*, etc.
- Have students choose two animal cards and make a list of ways in which they differ. Have them use a Venn diagram to organize their thoughts.

Answer Key

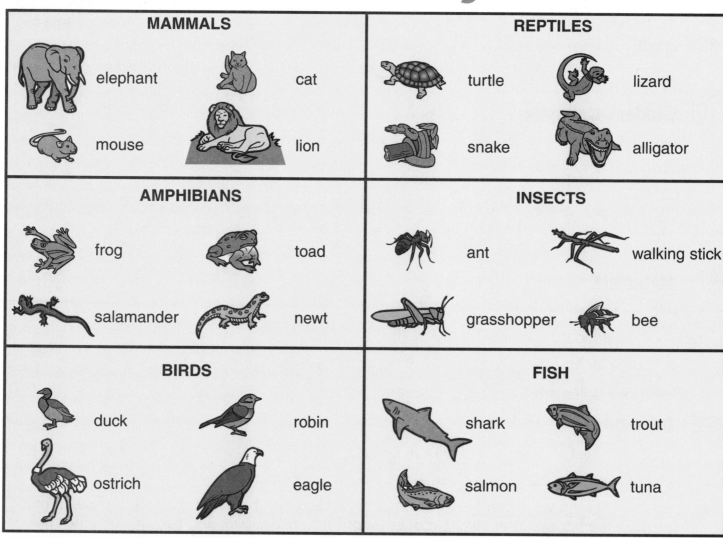

MAMMALS

elephant

cat

mouse

lion

REPTILES

turtle

lizard

snake

alligator

AMPHIBIANS

frog

toad

salamander

newt

INSECTS

ant

walking stick

grasshopper

bee

BIRDS

duck

robin

ostrich

eagle

FISH

shark

trout

salmon

tuna

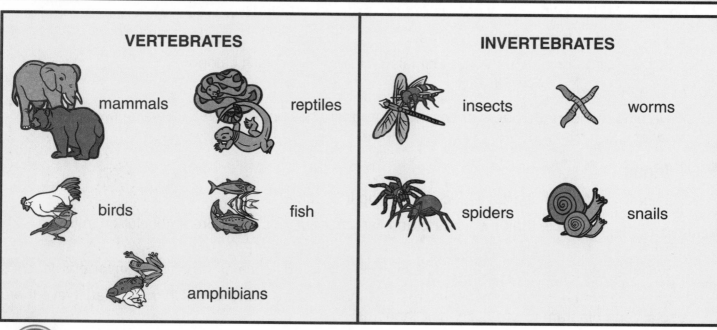

VERTEBRATES

mammals

reptiles

birds

fish

amphibians

INVERTEBRATES

insects

worms

spiders

snails

Mammal	Reptile
(Feeds its young milk and has hair or fur on its body)	(Has rough, dry scales or hard plates)
Amphibian	Insect
(Has wet skin and can live in both water and land)	(Has six legs, three body parts, and, sometimes, wings)
Bird	Fish
(Lays eggs and has feathers and wings)	(Lives in water and has fins and gills)

#3171 Science Literacy Activities

Animal Cards

elephant

mouse

cat

lion

turtle

snake

lizard

alligator

frog

salamander

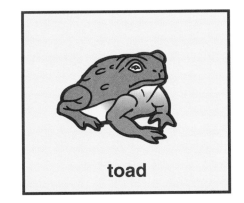
toad

newt

#3171 Science Literacy Activities

Animal Cards

ant

grasshopper

walking stick

bee

duck

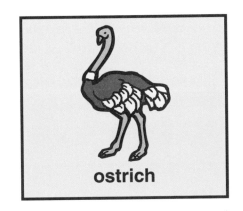
ostrich

robin

eagle

shark

salmon

trout

tuna

#3171 Science Literacy Activities

Invertebrates
(Animals without a Backbone)

Vertebrates
(Animals with a Backbone)

Animal Cards

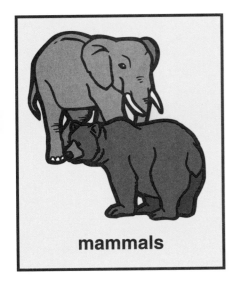

mammals

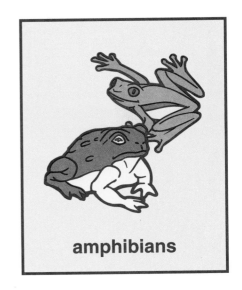

birds

amphibians

reptiles

fish

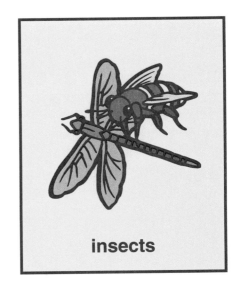

insects

spiders

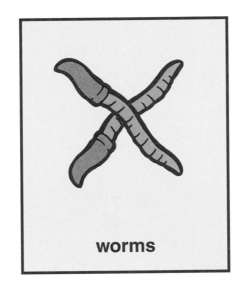

worms

snails

#3171 Science Literacy Activities

Cycle of Life

 Skill

- Identify the sequence of events of the life cycle of a plant, frog, or butterfly

 Student Grouping

- center
- independent
- whole group (*Note:* You must copy a Life Cycle Chart and set of cards for every student.)
- small group (*Note:* You must copy a Life Cycle Chart and set of cards for every student.)
- partners (*Note:* You must copy a Life Cycle Chart and set of cards for every set of partners.)

 Materials

- Life Cycle Chart (page 77)
- one set of cards (butterfly on page 79, frog on page 81, or plant on page 83)
- chalkboard or whiteboard
- Answer Key (page 76)
- chalk or whiteboard markers

 Directions

1. Write on the board the words *kitten* and *cat*.
2. Draw a picture of a kitten and cat next to the words. (*Note:* Use magazine pictures if you have difficulty drawing.)
3. Ask the students the difference between the two and brainstorm with students other names of young animals and matching names of the adult animals. Some examples are as follows: a cub and a lion or a pup and a dog.
4. Tell students that animals and plants grow and change. Tell them that parts of an animal's or plant's life are called its *life cycle*. It is the way an animal and a plant grow and change.
5. Tell students that they will put in order an animal's or plant's life cycle using cards.
6. Give each student a Life Cycle Chart and one set of animal (or plant) cards.
7. Have students mix the cards up and then place them in order on the chart. (*Note:* If you made copies of the chart and cards, you might ask students to glue their cards onto the chart and keep it as a reference.)
8. Have students read the chart to their friends when they are finished. (*Note:* Check with Answer Key.)

 Ideas

- Laminate the Life Cycle Chart and cards for durability, especially when used in a center.
- Store each of the life cycle cards in small, labeled, plastic bags.
- When implementing the activity on the bean plant, have students grow their own bean plants. Have students record their observations of each stage in a plant journal.
- Make several copies of the Life Cycle Chart. Have each student draw a life cycle on the blank chart (Examples: themselves or a pet). Then have each student write a paragraph using their charts. Have them use sequence words, such as *first*, *second*, and *last*. For example, one student might write, "This is my life cycle. First, I was born from my mother. Second, ..."

Life Cycle of a Butterfly

1
The butterfly lays eggs.

2
A caterpillar hatches from the egg.

5
The butterfly breaks open the chrysalis and flies away.

3
The caterpillar eats and starts to grow.

4
The caterpillar wraps itself in a chrysalis. It begins to change into a butterfly.

Life Cycle of a Frog

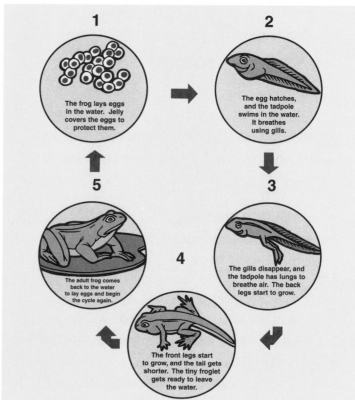

1
The frog lays eggs in the water. Jelly covers the eggs to protect them.

2
The egg hatches, and the tadpole swims in the water. It breathes using gills.

5
The adult frog comes back to the water to lay eggs and begin the cycle again.

3
The gills disappear, and the tadpole has lungs to breathe air. The back legs start to grow.

4
The front legs start to grow, and the tail gets shorter. The tiny froglet gets ready to leave the water.

Life Cycle of a Plant

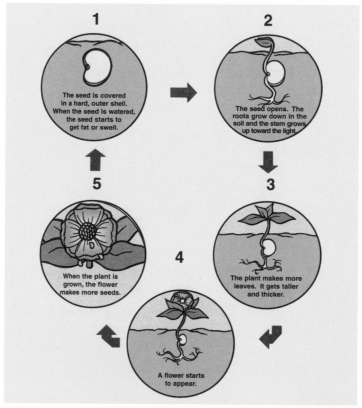

1
The seed is covered in a hard, outer shell. When the seed is watered, the seed starts to get fat or swell.

2
The seed opens. The roots grow down in the soil and the stem grows up toward the light.

5
When the plant is grown, the flower makes more seeds.

3
The plant makes more leaves. It gets taller and thicker.

4
A flower starts to appear.

Life Cycle Chart

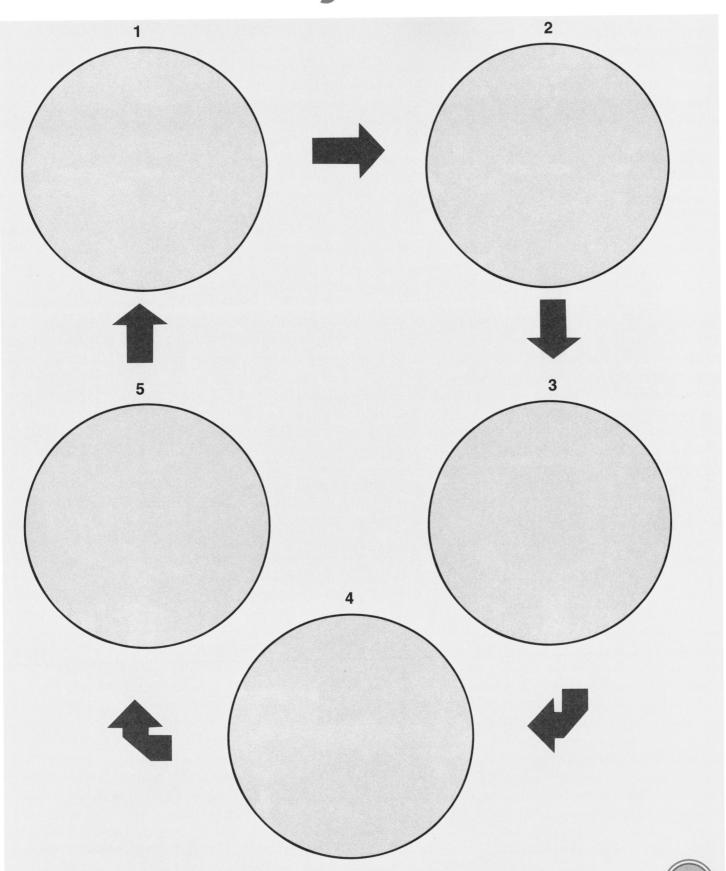

78

Butterfly Life Cycle (Cards)

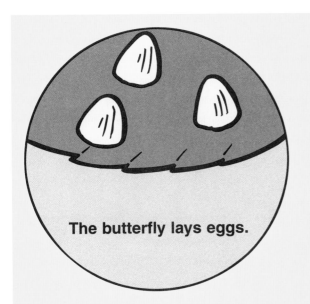

The butterfly lays eggs.

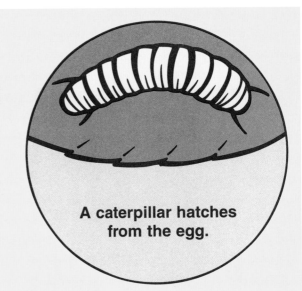

A caterpillar hatches from the egg.

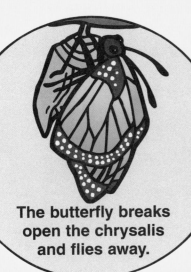

The butterfly breaks open the chrysalis and flies away.

The caterpillar eats and starts to grow.

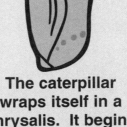

The caterpillar wraps itself in a chrysalis. It begins to change into a butterfly.

#3171 Science Literacy Activities

Frog Life Cycle (Cards)

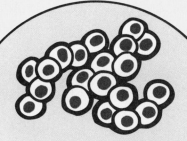

The frog lays eggs in the water. Jelly covers the eggs to protect them.

The egg hatches, and the tadpole swims in the water. It breathes using gills.

The adult frog comes back to the water to lay eggs and begin the cycle again.

The gills disappear, and the tadpole has lungs to breathe air. The back legs start to grow.

The front legs start to grow, and the tail gets shorter. The tiny froglet gets ready to leave the water.

Plant Life Cycle (Cards)

The seed is covered in a hard, outer shell. When the seed is watered, the seed starts to get fat or swell.

The seed opens. The roots grow down in the soil and the stem grows up toward the light.

When the plant is grown, the flower makes more seeds.

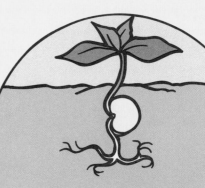

The plant makes more leaves. It gets taller and thicker.

A flower starts to appear.

A Body of Vocabulary

 Skill

- Understand the basic functions of the different parts of the body

Student Grouping

- large group (See note below in Directions #6.)
- small group
- partners
- center
- independent

Materials

- Body Vocabulary Cards (pages 87 and 89)
- Answer Key (page 86)

Directions

1. Mix cards up.
2. Lay the cards facedown on a flat surface.
3. The first player picks two cards.
4. Students read the cards together. If it is a match, the player keeps the two cards. If it is not a match, the player places the cards facedown.
5. The next player takes his or her turn.
6. The game finishes when all matches have been made. (*Note:* If playing in a large group, make copies of page 87. Hand a copy to each student. The teacher or a fluent reader can read the definition cards. Each player can place a marker on the body part when its definition is called.)
7. Use the Answer Key to check for correct definitions.

Ideas

- Laminate the vocabulary cards for durability, especially when using in a center.
- Prior to the activity, read books about the body. When students are playing, have the books about the body near the activity for student reference.
- Invite students to add more body parts to the set (picture card and definition card).
- Make a book about parts of the body. Have each student pick one body part, draw a picture of it, and write a few sentences about it. Make a cover and staple all the student pages to it. Then put it in your classroom library. Encourage students to do some research before writing and drawing their pages.

Answer Key

 brain: This part, in your head, controls how you think and move.

 skull: This bony part protects the brain.

 ribs: This part curves from the spine to the front of the chest and protects organs such as the heart.

 heart: This part pumps blood to all parts of your body.

 lungs: This part helps you breathe in oxygen.

 mouth: This part has saliva and teeth to help to break down the food.

 skeleton: This part is made up of 206 bones that hold up your body.

 muscle: This part is in between your skin and bones and helps you move.

 esophagus: This part moves the food from your mouth to your stomach.

 stomach: In this part, food mixes with special juices and turns it into a liquid.

 small intestine: The food liquid from the stomach moves into this part.

 large intestine: This part moves food that your body does not need.

#3171 Science Literacy Activities

Body Vocabulary Cards

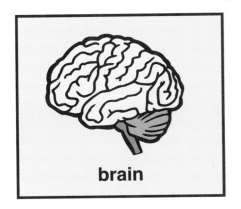

brain

skull

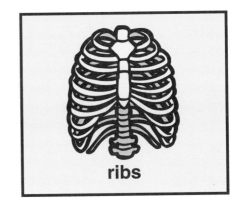

ribs

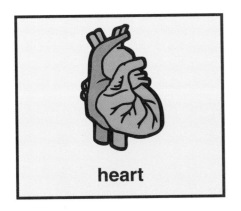

heart

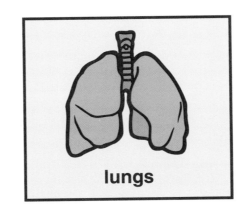

lungs

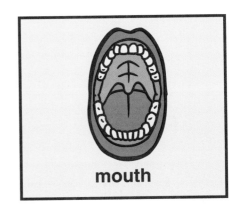

mouth

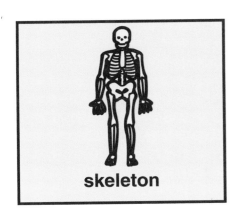

skeleton

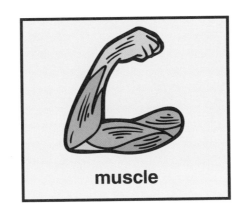

muscle

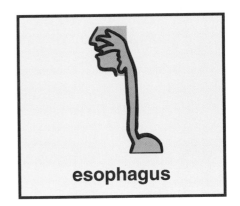

esophagus

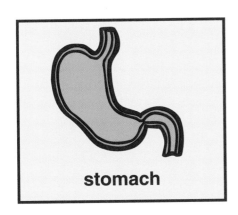

stomach

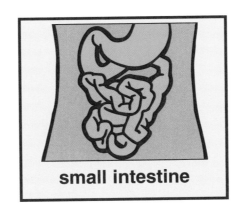

small intestine

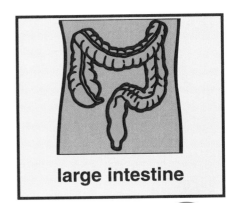

large intestine

#3171 Science Literacy Activities

Body Vocabulary Cards

This part, in your head, controls how you think and move.

This bony part protects the brain.

This part curves from the spine to the front of the chest and protects organs such as the heart.

This part pumps blood to all parts of your body.

This part helps you breathe in oxygen.

This part has saliva and teeth to help to break down the food.

This part is made up of 206 bones that hold up your body.

This part is in between your skin and bones and helps you move.

This part moves the food from your mouth to your stomach.

In this part, food mixes with special juices and turns it into a liquid.

The food liquid from the stomach moves into this part.

This part moves food that your body does not need.

#3171 Science Literacy Activities

Let the Rain Flow

EARTH SCIENCE

Skill

- Using a flow chart, identify that rain forms from water drops in clouds.

Student Grouping

- whole group (Make multiple copies of Water Cycle Flow Chart and the Water Cycle Stages.)
- small group (Make multiple copies of Water Cycle Flow Chart and the Water Cycle Stages.)
- partners (Make multiple copies of Water Cycle Flow Chart and the Water Cycle Stages.)
- center (See note below in #9 of Directions.)

Materials

- chalkboard or whiteboard
- chalk or whiteboard markers
- Water Cycle Flow Chart (page 93)
- Water Cycle Stages (page 95)
- Answer Key (page 92)

Directions

1. Draw a web on the board. Place the word *rain* in the center circle.
2. Brainstorm with students any facts they know about rain.
3. Explain to students that clouds are made up of many tiny drops of water, and when the cloud gets too heavy, the water drops fall as rain.
4. Hand students the Water Cycle Flow Chart and the cards on the Water Cycle Stages.
5. Have students mix up the circular cards that describe the stages of the water cycle.
6. Start with the *evaporation* stage of the water cycle. Read the card together. Answer any student questions about evaporation.
7. Have students put the card displaying the evaporation stage of the water cycle on the first space on the flow chart.
8. Tell students the next stage is *condensation*. Read the card together. Answer any student questions.
9. Continue going through the rest of the cards. (*Note:* You may choose to put the flow chart and circular cards at a center for students to read together, discuss, and figure out which stage is next. Have them use the Answer Key to verify their guesses.)

Ideas

- Laminate circular cards and chart, especially when using for a center.
- Have students keep a daily weather journal. Have them observe and describe the clouds, temperature, etc. Have them use words such as *sunny, windy,* or *rainy.*
- Bring in the weather section from newspapers. Help students understand temperature readings on a thermometer.

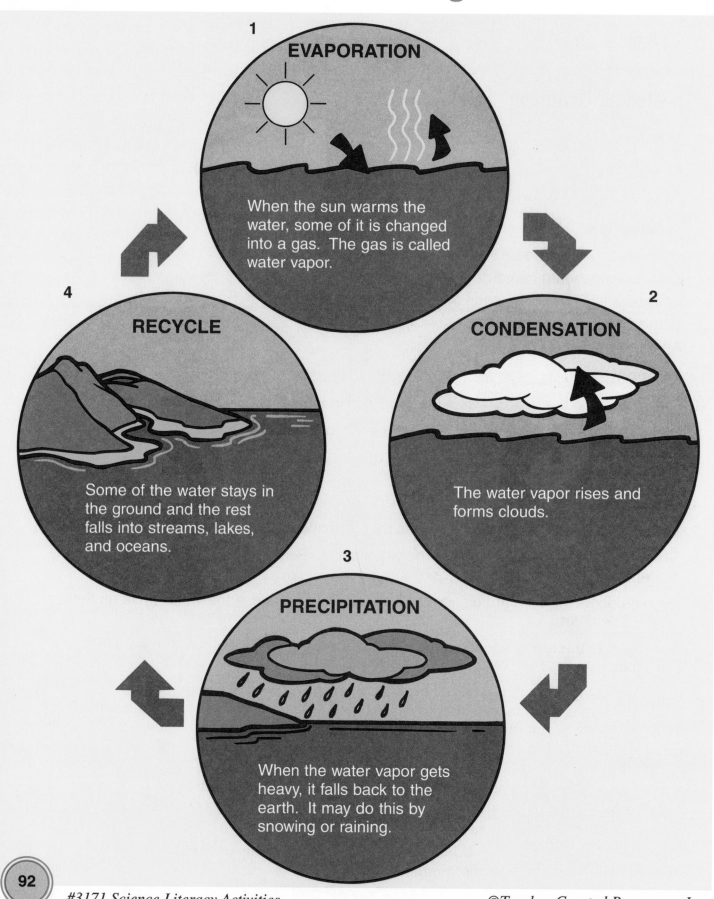

1

EVAPORATION

When the sun warms the water, some of it is changed into a gas. The gas is called water vapor.

4

RECYCLE

Some of the water stays in the ground and the rest falls into streams, lakes, and oceans.

2

CONDENSATION

The water vapor rises and forms clouds.

3

PRECIPITATION

When the water vapor gets heavy, it falls back to the earth. It may do this by snowing or raining.

#3171 Science Literacy Activities

©*Teacher Created Resources, Inc.*

Water Cycle Flow Chart

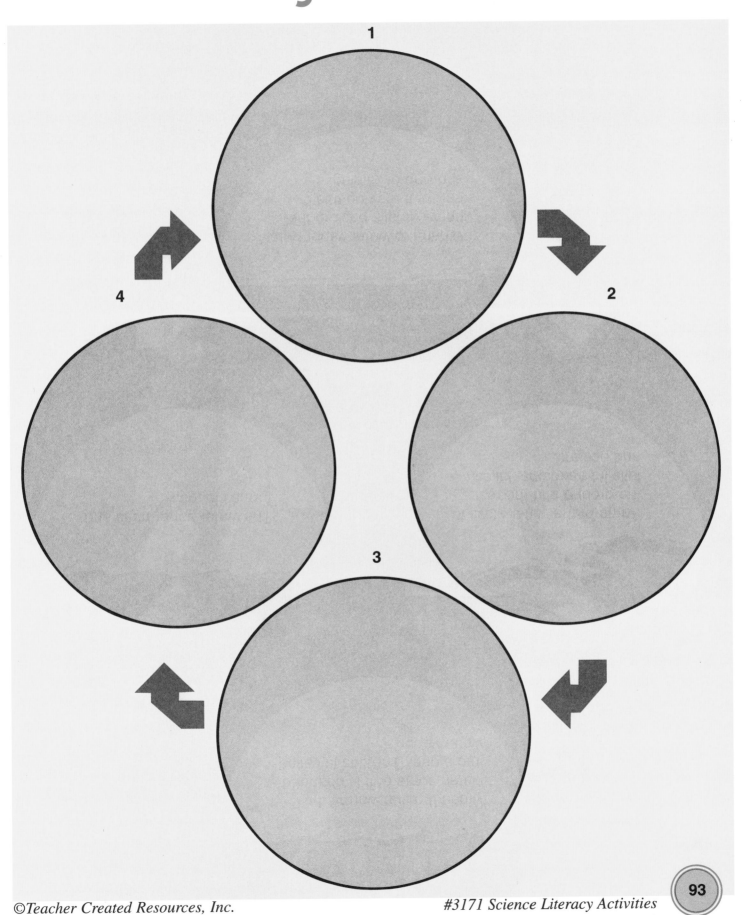

Water Cycle Stages

EVAPORATION

When the sun warms the water, some of it is changed into a gas. The gas is called water vapor.

RECYCLE

Some of the water stays in the ground and the rest falls into streams, lakes, and oceans.

CONDENSATION

The water vapor rises and forms clouds.

PRECIPITATION

When the water vapor gets heavy, it falls back to the earth. It may do this by snowing or raining.

©*Teacher Created Resources, Inc.* *#3171 Science Literacy Activities*

#3171 Science Literacy Activities ©*Teacher Created Resources, Inc.*

A Sequence of Seasons

 Skill

- Recognize the sequence of seasons and what activities happen in each season

 Student Grouping

- whole group
- small group

 Materials

- Season Titles (page 99)
- pictures of the seasons (pages 101–107)
- Answer Key (page 98)

 Directions

1. Tell students that seasons are times of the year and that the seasons have a special order.

2. Show the students the picture cards. Have them study each one.

3. Tell students that you need help placing them in order.

4. Mount or tape the spring picture on a board or wall for all to see. Ask a student to place the proper title card above the picture.

5. Continue with students to place the rest of the picture cards and title cards in the appropriate order. (See Answer Key on page 98.)

6. Tell students that now the seasons are in order, you have some questions to ask them. They must guess what season answers the question.

7. Ask students questions from page 98.

 Ideas

- Laminate the picture and title cards for durability.

- As a closing activity, have students write the title of each season on a piece of paper. Then write and/or draw activities that happen in each season.

- Have students make a book about seasons.

- On a calendar, keep track of when seasons change and when the daylight starts to change.

- Have each student pick a season and make a collage, depicting that season, using magazine pictures.

- Use the titles and picture cards to make a bulletin board display titled, "Sequence of Seasons."

- Have students make paper dolls and dress them according to season or cut out magazine pictures of clothing and sort by season.

Answer Key

Sequence of Seasons

Questions About Seasons

- What season is a good time to plant seeds? (spring)
- What season comes after spring? (summer)
- What season has more daylight than any other season? (summer)
- In what season does it start to cool down? (fall)
- What season first starts to get more daylight? (spring)
- In what season does the air start to get really hot? (summer)
- In what season do plants get less sunlight and stop growing bigger? (fall)
- In what season do animals usually start to store food? (fall)
- In what season does the air get cold and snow starts to fall in many places? (winter)
- In what season does the rain help the seeds grow? (spring)
- What season comes after summer? (fall)
- In what season are many plants and trees bare? (winter)
- In what season do many fruits grow? (summer)
- In what season do you start to get fewer hours of daylight? (fall)
- In what season do many animals have babies? (spring)
- What season comes after fall? (winter)
- In what season do the leaves change colors in some places? (fall)
- What season comes after winter? (spring)

#3171 Science Literacy Activities

SPRING

SUMMER

FALL

WINTER

#3171 Science Literacy Activities

Fascinating Fossils

Skill

- Understand how fossils are made and how scientists collect fossils

Student Grouping

- small group
- center
- whole group (Copy the page of Fossil Cards for each student.)
- independent
- partners

Materials

- chalkboard or whiteboard
- chalk or whiteboard markers
- Fossil Cards (page 111)
- Fascinating Fossils Recording Sheet (page 110)
- Answer Key (page 113)

Directions

1. Explain to students that plants and animals lived on Earth a long time ago, before people did. Scientists know this because they have found fossils. Tell students that a fossil is what is left of a plant or animal that lived a long time ago.

2. On the board, using pictures and words, explain to students one possible way of becoming a fossil: (a) An animal or plant dies. (b) Then mud or sand covers the plant or animal. (c) The plant or animal remains pressed on the mud for a long time until the mud becomes rock. (d) An imprint of the plant or animal is left in the rock. (*Note:* You may want to demonstrate the imprinting process with a shell and piece of clay or playdough.)

3. Explain to students that when scientists find a fossil, they must remove the fossil from the rock very carefully and very slowly so as not to break it.

4. Tell students that today they will become paleontologists, scientists who find and study fossils.

5. Hand each student a copy of the Fascinating Fossil Recording Sheet.

6. Tell them that they must study each fossil card and identify the fossil.

7. They must record their findings on the recording sheet. Tell students to make sure to match their answers to the correct card number.

8. Have students check their answers against the Answer Key.

Ideas

- Laminate fossil cards, especially if using in a center.
- Have students make imprints with a variety of objects, such as shells, in clay or playdough.
- Have students make their own books about fossils (explaining what a paleontologist is, summarizing the processes of becoming a fossil, telling what kind of plants and animals have become fossils, etc.).
- At a center, for added excitement, hide fossil cards in a box filled with sand. Have students dig for the cards.

Fascinating Fossils Recording Sheet

1. _____

2. _____

3. _____

4. _____

5. _____

6. _____

7. _____

8. _____

9. _____

10. _____

11. _____

12. _____

#3171 Science Literacy Activities

Fossil Cards

1.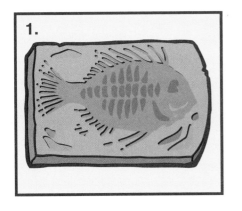

2.

3.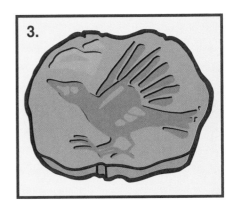

4.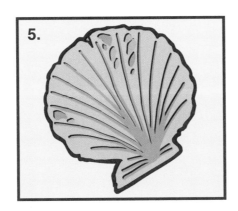

5.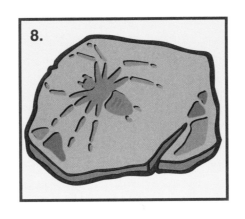

6.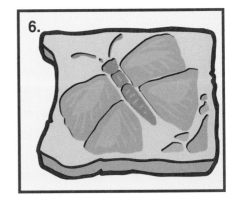

7.

8.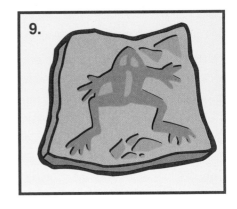

9.

10.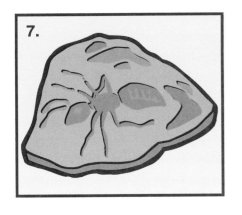

11.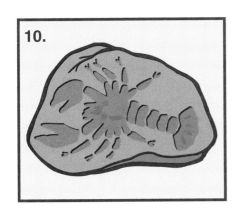

12.

Answer Key

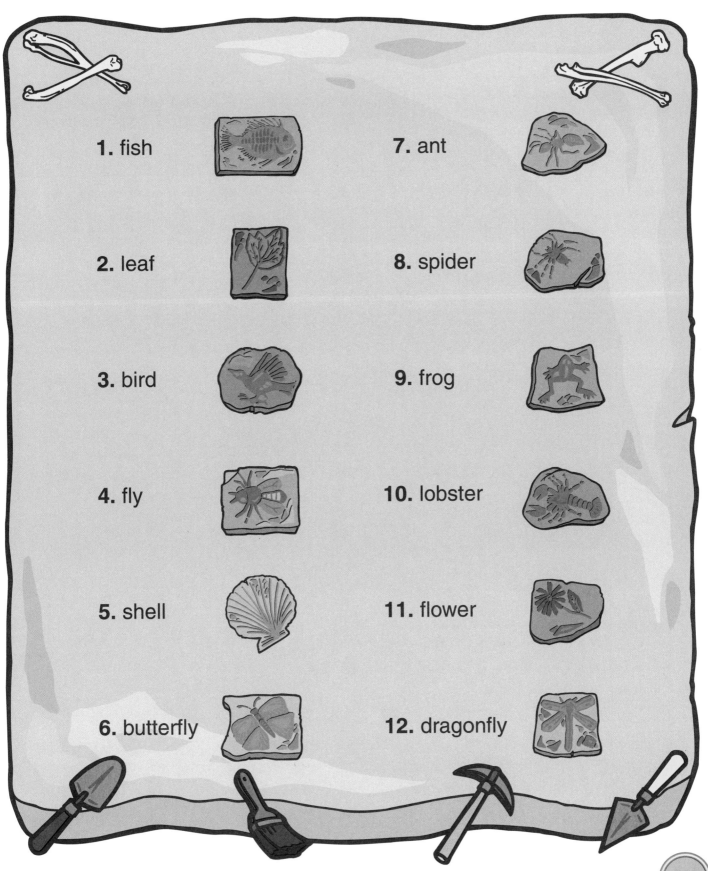

1. fish

2. leaf

3. bird

4. fly

5. shell

6. butterfly

7. ant

8. spider

9. frog

10. lobster

11. flower

12. dragonfly

#3171 Science Literacy Activities

#3171 Science Literacy Activities

Data to Dinosaur

 Skill

- Identify different kinds of dinosaurs and what facts scientists have learned about them

 Student Grouping

- whole group
- small group
- center

 Materials

- chalkboard or whiteboard
- chalk or whiteboard markers
- Dinosaur Fact Cards (pages 117 and 119)
- dinosaur pictures (pages 121 through 141)
- Answer Key (page 116)

 Directions

1. Find out what students already know about dinosaurs and record their answers on the board.
2. Post the dinosaur pictures so students can see all of them.
3. Tell students that dinosaurs are animals that lived millions of years ago.
4. Tell them that the dinosaurs are extinct, which means they are no longer alive today. Tell them, also, that paleontologists can find out a lot about the dinosaurs from their fossils.
5. Go over the names of each dinosaur. Ask students to make brief observations about each picture.
6. Explain that today they are going to help you match some facts to the dinosaur pictures. (*Note:* Check answers with Answer Key.)
7. Mix up the fact cards.
8. Ask students under which dinosaur picture the fact card should be placed.
9. As a class or a small group, match all fact cards to the dinosaur pictures.

 Ideas

- Laminate picture and facts cards for durability, especially if using in a center.
- Compile a book of dinosaur facts, having each student creating a dinosaur fact page.
- Use the dinosaur pictures and fact cards to create an interactive bulletin board where students match the facts cards to the pictures.
- Place students in groups and have each group research one dinosaur in depth. Have them write a summary of their findings.
- Classify the dinosaurs into the following categories: herbivores, carnivores, or both.

Answer Key

Tyrannosaurus rex

I am one of the largest meat-eating dinosaurs and walk upright on two strong, hind legs.
I have three-toed feet and two-fingered hands with claws.

Stegosaurus

I am known as the "plated lizard" because I have bony plates down my back.
My tail has four sharp spikes.

Triceratops

I am named "three-horned face."
I have two sharp horns over my eyes and one short horn on my nose.

Diplodocus

I am the longest dinosaur, and I eat plants and vegetables.
I have a long, whip-like tail that I sometimes use as a weapon.

Pteranodon

I am a flying reptile.
I have a bird-like beak with no teeth.

Elasmosaurus

I swim in warm oceans.
I have a long, thick neck, a short tail, and flippers shaped like paddles.

Spinosaurus

I have tall spines running down my back.
My name is "spiny lizard."

Velociraptor

I have a small body and strong legs built for running.
I have three-fingered hands and a sharp, curved claw on each foot.

Iguanodon

I have one sharp, pointed thumb on each hand.
My name is "iguana-tooth."

Ankylosaurus

I am covered with a bony, shell-like covering.
I have a thick club at the end of my tail.

Anatosaurus

My name means "duck lizard."
I have a flat head and a duck-bill.

#3171 Science Literacy Activities

Dinosaur Fact Cards

I am one of the largest meat-eating dinosaurs and walk upright on two strong, hind legs.

I have three-toed feet and two-fingered hands with claws.

I am known as the "plated lizard" because I have bony plates down my back.

My tail has four sharp spikes.

I am named "three-horned face."

I have two sharp horns over my eyes and one short horn on my nose.

I am the longest dinosaur, and I eat plants and vegetables.

I have a long, whip-like tail that I sometimes use as a weapon.

I am a flying reptile.

I have a bird-like beak with no teeth.

I swim in warm oceans.

I have a long, thick neck, a short tail, and flippers shaped like paddles.

Dinosaur Fact Cards

I have tall spines running down my back.

My name is "spiny lizard."

I have a small body and strong legs built for running.

I have three-fingered hands and a sharp, curved claw on each foot.

I have one sharp, pointed thumb on each hand.

My name is "iguana-tooth."

I am covered with a bony, shell-like covering.

I have a thick club at the end of my tail.

My name means "duck lizard."

I have a flat head and a duck-bill.

Tyrannosaurus rex

Stegosaurus

#3171 Science Literacy Activities

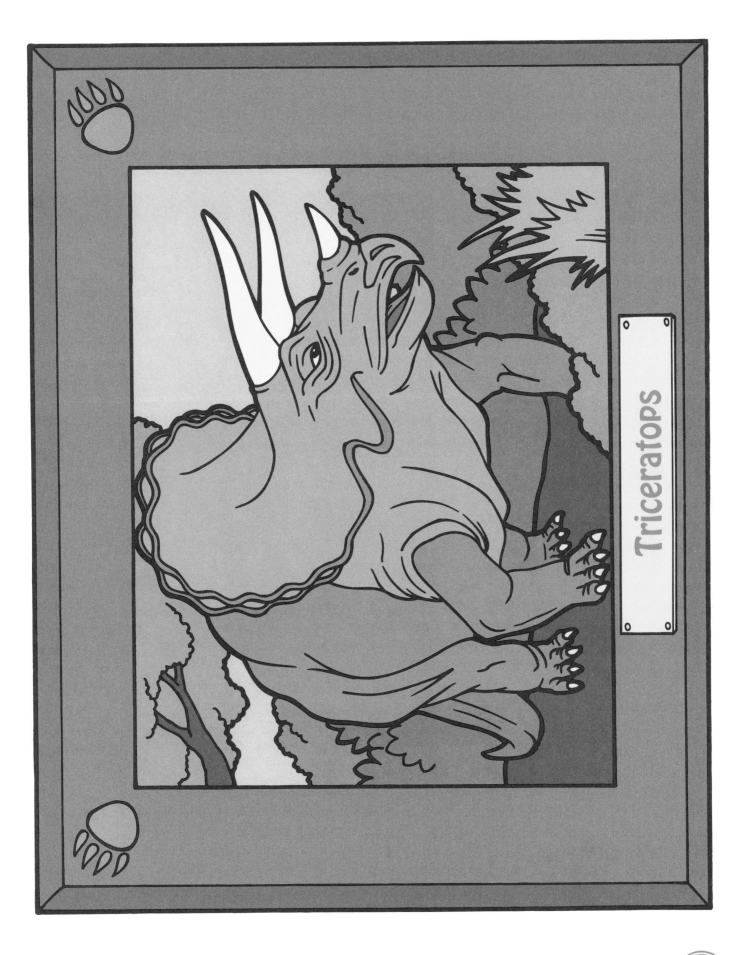

Triceratops

Diplodocus

Pteranodon

Elasmosaurus

#3171 Science Literacy Activities

Spinosaurus

#3171 Science Literacy Activities

©*Teacher Created Resources, Inc.*

Velociraptor

Iguanodon

#3171 Science Literacy Activities

©*Teacher Created Resources, Inc.*

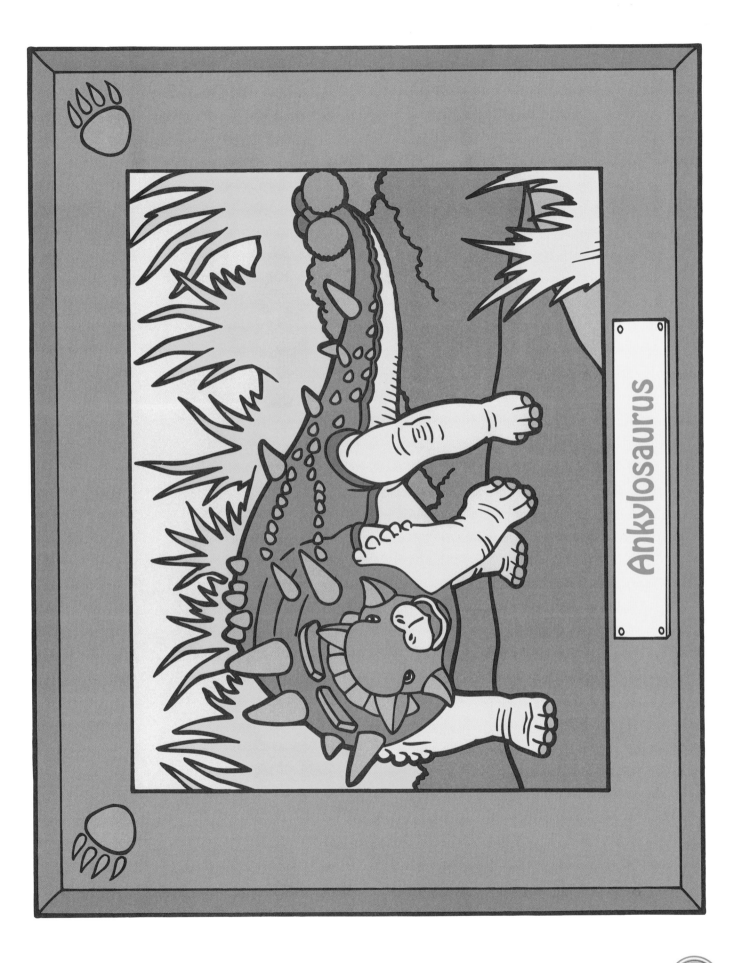

Ankylosaurus

Anatosaurus

Wonderfully Natural

 Skill

- Identify natural resources that people use

 Student Grouping

- whole group
- small group
- center

 Materials

- glass of water or water bottle filled with water
- objects that show natural resources (jewelry made from a rock, piece of fruit, etc.)
- chalkboard or whiteboard
- chalk or whiteboard markers
- picture cards (pages 145–151)

 Directions

1. Lay the objects that show natural resources in front of students.
2. Tell students that people use a lot of things made from nature to meet their needs.
3. Draw a web on the board. Write the words *natural resource* in the center of the web.
4. Tell them that a natural resource is anything from nature that people can use.
5. Drink some water from a water bottle or glass.
6. Ask students, "Does anybody know the natural resource I just used?" Students should answer, "Water."
7. Write the word *water* on the one of the lines on the web.
8. Have students identify the natural resources used by the other objects and add them to the web. Then brainstorm some additional things they use in the classroom that come from natural resources.
9. Show students one of the picture cards.
10. Ask students to describe each picture on the card. Then ask students what natural resource is being used in the pictures on the card (water, air, plants, or rocks, depending on what card you are using).
11. Repeat the process with the other picture cards.

 Ideas

- Laminate the picture cards for durability.
- Have students create their own picture cards that depict natural resources being used.
- Have students bring things from home from a natural resource. Have students give written and oral reports to the class identifying the natural resources and how they use them at home.
- Bring various rocks. Have students observe the size, shape, and texture. Discuss with them how rocks can be natural resources.

#3171 Science Literacy Activities

#3171 Science Literacy Activities

©*Teacher Created Resources, Inc.*

Categories of Matter

 Skill

- Identify objects as solid, liquid, or gas

 Student Grouping

- whole group
- small group
- center

- partners
- independent

 Materials

- chalkboard or whiteboard
- paper and writing utensils (Only if playing Option *a*. See below in Direction #5.)
- scissors (Only if playing Option *b*. See below in Direction #5.)

- chalk or whiteboard markers
- Sorting Board (page 155)
- Object Cards (page 157)
- Answer Key (page 154)

 Directions

1. Explain to students that all things are made of *matter*. For example, chair, juice, and the air in a tire are all made of matter. Tell them that even they are made of matter.

2. Write *solid*, *liquid*, and *gas* on the board.

3. Tell them that matter has three forms. It can be a solid that has a shape of its own, like a chair. It can be a liquid that flows and does not have its own shape, like the juice. Or, it can be a gas that fills all the space inside a container, like the air in a tire.

4. Have students brainstorm other objects that fit into each category.

5. Tell students that they will now play a game in which they need to figure out which object goes under what category. You may play the activity in one of the following ways: (a) As a whole group, have students write the three categories (solid, liquid, gas) on paper. Then the teacher or a student reads the name of the object on the Object Card. The students write the name of the object in one of the categories. When the object cards are finished, the Answer Key is read. The students check their answers. (b) Make copies of the Object Cards and Sorting Board for each student. Have students cut out their object cards. Have them mix the cards and place them in a pile. Tell them that you are going to time them. They must categorize their cards on the board as fast as possible. After time is up, read the Answer Key and have students check their answers. (c) They may sort the Object Cards on the Sorting Board independently or with partners at a center. Students can check the Answer Key against their answers.

 Ideas

- Laminate the Sorting Board and Object Cards, especially when using in a center.
- Have students bring in objects from home and sort them into the categories.
- Use water to illustrate the three forms of water (ice = solid, glass of water = liquid, steam from a boiling pot = gas).

Answer Key

Solid

 ball

 pencil

 eraser

 book

 tree

Liquid

 milk

 tar

 honey

 oil

 tea

Gas

 air in a balloon

 air in a bubble

 air in a ball

 car exhaust

 steam from an iron

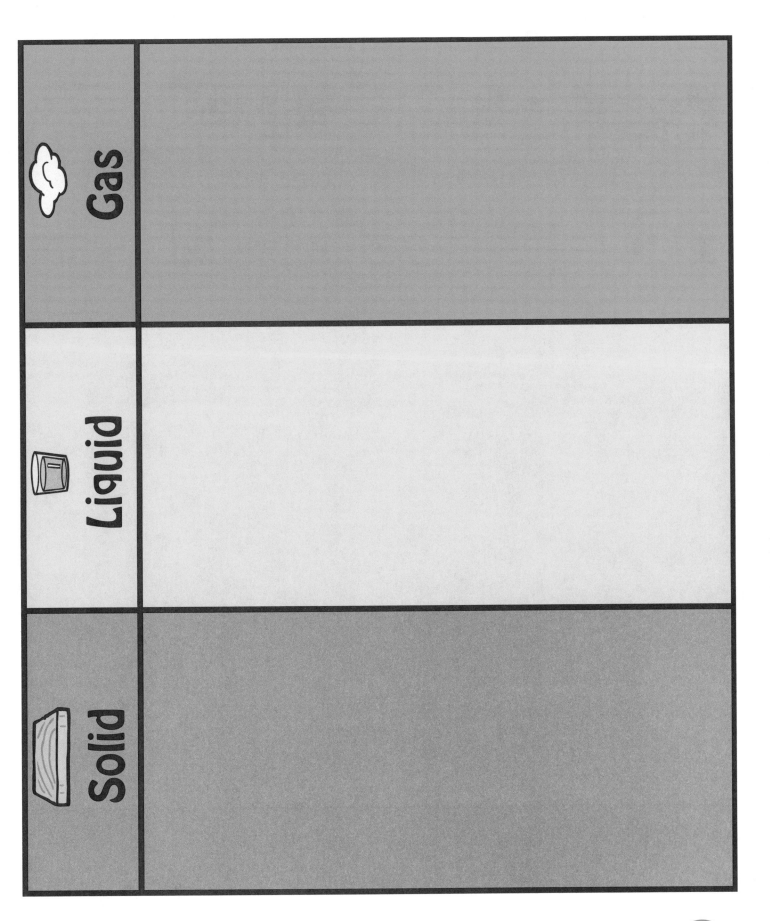

Object Cards

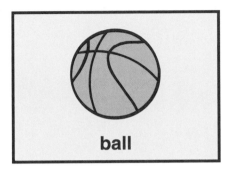

ball

pencil

tree

book

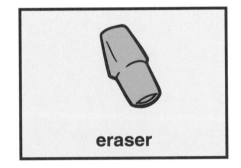

eraser

milk

tar

honey

oil

tea

air in a balloon

air in a bubble

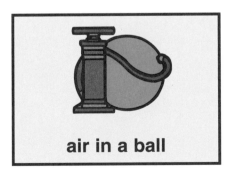

air in a ball

car exhaust

steam from an iron

#3171 Science Literacy Activities 1–2

A Magnificent Magnet

Skill

- Sort objects according to whether or not they are attracted by a magnet

Student Grouping

- whole group
- small group
- center
- partners
- independent

Materials

- magnet
- Mr. Magnet Board (page 161)
- Object Cards (page 163)
- Answer Key (page 160)
- scissors and glue (optional, See Option *a* below in Directions #5.)

Directions

1. Explain to students that a magnet is a piece of iron that can attract, or pull, things. (*Note:* Show a magnet to the students while explaining this.)

2. Tell them that it can only pull those things that are made of iron. (*Note:* Find something in the classroom that attracts the magnet and show the attraction to the students.)

3. Explain that iron is a kind of metal.

4. Ask students to name some magnets they used or saw and what they attracted. For example, some students may have magnets on their refrigerator doors.

5. Tell them that they will do an activity that requires them to find out what items will attract to a magnet. This activity can be implemented the following ways: (a) The Mr. Magnet Board and object cards can be copied and distributed to each student. They can cut out the cards and follow the directions independently. You may want to have them glue on the cards after you check their papers. (b) Leave the blank chart and object cards to be played at a center in partners, independently, or as a small group. (*Note:* You may wish to have a magnet and the actual items next to the chart so students can actually check to see whether the magnet is attracted to the item.)

6. Have students make predictions and discuss their guesses.

7. Students' answers are checked against the Answer Key.

Ideas

- Laminate Mr. Magnet Board and Object Cards for durability.

- Copy the Mr. Magnet Board. Have students write in the squares other items that attract the magnet or magnet facts.

- Bring in different sizes and shapes of magnets. Have students use them to hunt around the classroom for things to which the magnet is attracted. (*Note:* Caution students to *not* touch magnets to computers, recorders, watches, televisions, etc., as magnets can cause severe damage and ruin these items.)

- Have students place objects in a glass of water or above a piece of paper and see if the magnet will attract through the water or paper.

Answer Key

Mr. Magnet is attracted to the following objects:

 metal screw

 metal spoon

 staples

 metal whistle

 key

 metal toy car

 paper clip

 metal lunchbox

 needle

 metal scissors

Mr. Magnet Board

Directions: Mr. Magnet is only attracted to only 10 of the objects on the cards. Place the object cards, of objects to which you think Mr. Magnet will be attracted, on the chart.

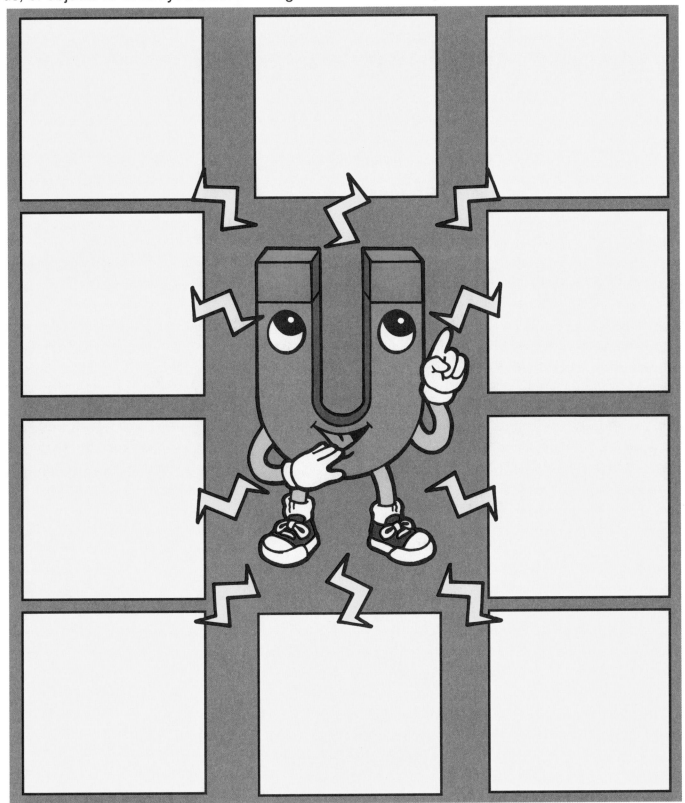

Object Cards

metal screw

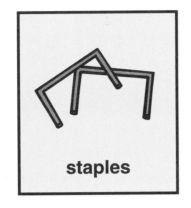

staples

rock

key

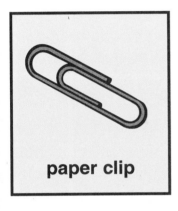

paper clip

rubber band

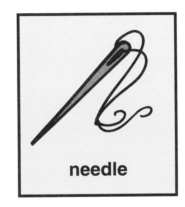

needle

metal spoon

leaf

metal whistle

metal toy car

metal lunchbox

crayon

metal scissors

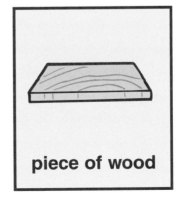

piece of wood

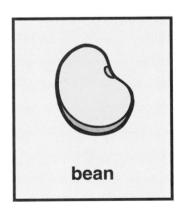

bean

#3171 Science Literacy Activities

#3171 Science Literacy Activities

Sink or Float Vote

PHYSICAL SCIENCE

Skill

- Understand that some objects sink and others may float in water

Student Grouping

- whole group (See #6 option a.)
- small group (See #6 option a.)
- partners (See #6 option b.)
- independent (See #6 option b.)

Materials

- chalkboard or whiteboard
- chalk or whiteboard markers
- a variety of objects that will sink and float—sponge, pencil, marble, etc.
- craft sticks
- Voting Signs (pages 167 through 175)
- Sink or Float Recording Sheet (page 166)
- aquarium filled with water
- glue or tape

Directions

1. Explain to students that some objects stay on top of a liquid or float and some objects drop to the bottom of a liquid or sink. Tell them they can also change the shape of the object to make it sink or float.

2. Tell students that we can make guesses or predictions about which objects will sink and which objects will float.

3. Test one object with students. Write the name of the object on the board.

4. Then write the word *Prediction* next to the name of the object. Ask students to make a prediction or guess about the object. Will it sink? Or will it float? Discuss why they think the object will sink or float. Write their predictions on the board.

5. Test the object in the water. Write the word *Result* next to their predictions. Write the actual result of the test. Compare the predictions and actual result with the students. Were they the same? Different? Why?

6. The next part of the activity can be implemented in the following ways: (a) Hand out a Sink and a Float sign to each student. (*Note:* Glue or tape a craft stick to each sign prior to the activity.) In front of the class, test each item. However, before you test an object, take a vote. Tell them to raise their Sink signs if they think the object will sink or raise their Float signs if they think the object will float. Tally the votes and then compare the numbers. Test the item and discuss the results. (b) At a center, leave copies of the Sink or Float Recording Sheet by an aquarium with objects around it for them to test. Tell them to record the names of their objects, their predictions, and the actual results on the sheet.

Ideas

- Laminate the voting signs before gluing or taping craft sticks to them.
- Have students take home a Sink or Float Recording Sheet and test some items at home.
- Have students make a book titled, *Sink or Float*.
- As a challenge, have students write words to describe the properties that make objects sink or float.

Sink or Float Recording Sheet

Directions: Write the name of the object you are going to test. Next, make a prediction or guess—*sink* or *float*. Then write the actual result of your test—*sink* or *float*.

Object: _____ Prediction (Guess): _____ Result: _____

Object: _____ Prediction (Guess): _____ Result: _____

Object: _____ Prediction (Guess): _____ Result: _____

Object: _____ Prediction (Guess): _____ Result: _____

Object: _____ Prediction (Guess): _____ Result: _____

Object: _____ Prediction (Guess): _____ Result: _____

Object: _____ Prediction (Guess): _____ Result: _____

Object: _____ Prediction (Guess): _____ Result: _____

Object: _____ Prediction (Guess): _____ Result: _____

Object: _____ Prediction (Guess): _____ Result: _____

#3171 Science Literacy Activities

#3171 Science Literacy Activities

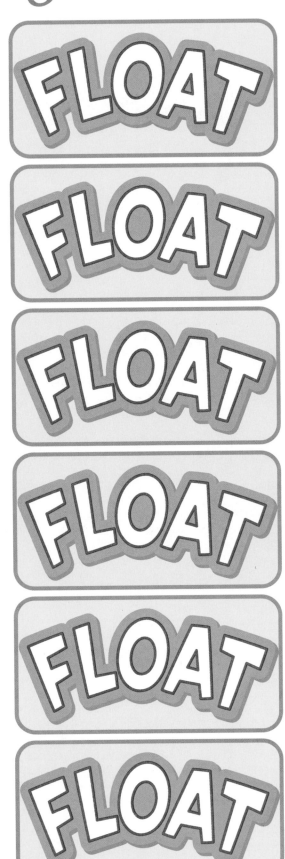

Voting Signs

#3171 Science Literacy Activities